Summer Success®
Math

Patsy F. Kanter • Leigh E. Palmer • Shara S. Hammet

GReaT SouRCe®
EDUCATION GROUP
A Houghton Mifflin Company

Credits

Design/Production: Taurins Design

Illustration Credits: Rusty Fletcher *pages 71, 77, 83.* **Jackie Snider** *pages 4, 5, 6, 58, 85, 98, 99, 100, 101.*

International Standard Book Number: 0-669-47850-4

3 4 5 6 7 8 9 10   MZ   05 04 03 02

Visit our web site: http://www.greatsource.com/

Name _____

Choose the best answer for each question.

1. What number do the base ten materials represent?

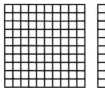

220   218   217   208
○   ○   ○   ○

2. What number is the same as four hundred five?

4005   450   415   405
○   ○   ○   ○

3. What is the value of the 4 in 846?

○ 4 ones   ○ 4 hundreds

○ 4 tens   ○ 4 thousands

4. Which number has a 5 in the hundreds place?

356   635   536   655
○   ○   ○   ○

5. What number is 100 more than 653?

653   654   663   753
○   ○   ○   ○

6. Which group of numbers is in order from least to greatest?

○ 291, 292, 294, 293

○ 153, 155, 159, 157

○ 432, 434, 436, 438

○ 549, 547, 545, 543

7. Which statement is true?

○ 256 > 258

○ 288 > 278

○ 222 < 222

○ 198 = 189

8. Circle the tenth heart.

♥ ♥ ♥ ♥ ♥ ♥ ♥ ♥ ♥ ♥ ♥ ♥

9. Which picture shows 1 out of 3 equal parts shaded?

10. What is the missing number in the number pattern?

110, 120, 130, 140, ☐ ,160, 170,...

141   145   150   155
○   ○   ○   ○

11. I am a whole number less than 10. Add 3 to me and get 8. Which number line has a star on me?

○ ← | | | ★ | | | | | | | | →
     0 1 2 3 4 5 6 7 8 9 10

○ ← | | | | | | | | ★ | | →
     0 1 2 3 4 5 6 7 8 9 10

○ ← | | | | | ★ | | | | | →
     0 1 2 3 4 5 6 7 8 9 10

○ ← | | | | ★ | | | | | | →
     0 1 2 3 4 5 6 7 8 9 10

12. Which is a set of odd numbers?

○ 6 8 12   ○ 5 10 11

○ 3 9 13   ○ 6 9 13

13. Which number sentence is in the same family of facts as $17 - 8$?

○ $17 + 8 = 25$

○ $17 + 9 = 26$

○ $8 + 8 = 16$

○ $8 + 9 = 17$

14. About how many paper clips long is the pencil?

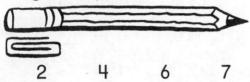

2   4   6   7
○   ○   ○   ○

15. Fred has these coins in his pocket. How much money does he have?

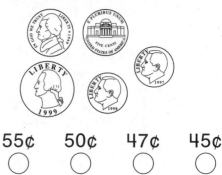

55¢   50¢   47¢   45¢
○   ○   ○   ○

16. Jakira has 36 baseball cards in her collection. Mateo has 8 more cards than Jakira in his collection. How many baseball cards does Mateo have?

28   32   34   44
○   ○   ○   ○

17. $7 + 75 =$ _____

18. $42 - 18 =$ _____

19. $235 + 68 =$ _____

20.
$$\begin{array}{r} 15 \\ 39 \\ + 51 \\ \hline \end{array}$$

21. $5 \times 3 =$ _____

22. What time is shown on the clock?

2:40   2:45   3:40   3:45
◯   ◯   ◯   ◯

23. Look at the figures in the box.

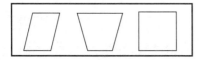

Which figure belongs to this group?

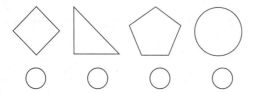

◯   ◯   ◯   ◯

24. Which object is shaped like a cylinder?

◯   ◯   ◯   ◯

25. The table shows the favorite pizza of some second-grade students. Which graph matches the facts given in the table?

Kind of Pizza	Number of Students
Cheese	7
Pepperoni	11
Sausage	6

◯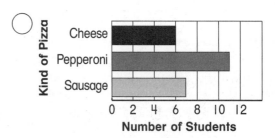

◯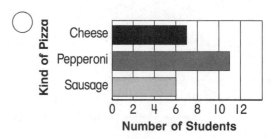

◯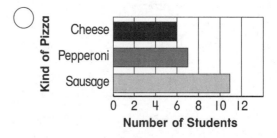

◯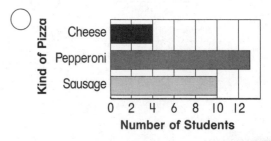

26. What is the date of the next Sunday on this calendar page?

JULY						
Sun.	Mon.	Tues.	Wed.	Thur.	Fri.	Sat.
		1	2	3	4	5
6	7	8	9	10	11	12
13						

14	15	19	20
○	○	○	○

27. Paloma is 2 inches taller than Dolores. Dolores is 3 inches taller than Darence. Darence is 1 inch taller than Zoe. Which child is the shortest?

○ Paloma   ○ Dolores

○ Darence   ○ Zoe

28. Theo has read 15 pages in his book. He still has 18 pages to read. How many pages are in the book?

23	25	32	33
○	○	○	○

29. Oreana feeds her fish 3 times each week. Which of the following could be used to find how many times she feeds her fish in 3 weeks?

○ $3 + 3$ ○ 3×3

○ $3 - 3$ ○ $3 \div 3$

30. There are 6 pieces of gum in a package. How many pieces of gum will Indra and her friend get if they share the gum equally?

6	5	4	3
○	○	○	○

31. Allen had $20. He spent $5 on crayons and $8 for a book. Which method could be used to find how much money he has left?

○ Add $20, $5, and $8.

○ Add $8 and $5 and then subtract $20.

○ Add $8 and $5 and then subtract that amount from $20.

○ Subtract $20, $5, and $8.

Name _____

First, draw a box around the problems that will have even answers. Then solve the problems.

1. $2 + 1 =$ _____   2. $5 - 1 =$ _____   3. $4 + 1 =$ _____

4. $9 - 1 =$ _____   5. $8 + 1 =$ _____   6. $6 + 1 =$ _____

7. $7 - 1 =$ _____   8. $10 - 1 =$ _____   9. $8 - 1 =$ _____

Write a number sentence to solve this story problem. Tell how you got your answer.

10. Billy has 9 stuffed animals. 5 of the stuffed animals are bears and the rest are frogs. How many of the stuffed animals are frogs?

_____

_____

_____

 DRAW

 WRITE

_____

_____

_____

_____

First, draw a box around the problems that will
have even answers. Then solve the problems.

1. 3 + 2 = _____   **2.** 4 − 2 = _____   **3.** 6 − 2 = _____

4. 8 + 2 = _____   **5.** 12 − 2 = _____   **6.** 9 − 2 = _____

7. 7 + 2 = _____   **8.** 2 + 6 = _____   **9.** 5 + 2 = _____

Draw an ABAB pattern here. Use squares and triangles.

10. _____

Draw an AABAAB pattern here. Use circles and squares.

11. _____

 DRAW    WRITE

_____

_____

_____

_____

Fast Facts Match-Up

Fast Facts Match-Up

Fast Facts Match-Up

Fast Facts
Match-Up

| 2 | 3 | 4 | 5 |

| 6 | 7 | 8 | 9 | 10 |

| 11 | 12 | 13 | 14 | 15 |

| 16 | 17 | 18 | 19 |

Get the Total

MATERIALS

2 sets of Ten Grid Cards cardstock (40 cards)

DIRECTIONS

1. Make a recording sheet like the one shown below. Shuffle the cards and place them facedown in a pile on the table.

2. The object is to add two or more cards to make each target total in order from 6 to 12. Player 1 turns over two cards. If the two cards make the target total, the player states the addition sentence, writes the number sentence on the recording sheet, and takes the cards. Player 2 then turns over two more cards and tries to make the next higher target total.

3. If the two cards do not make the target total, Player 2 turns over the next card from the facedown pile and tries to make the target total using all the cards, or any combination of turned over cards. If the total can be made, Player 2 states the number sentence, writes it on the recording sheet, and takes the cards.

4. If the cards do not make the target total, play passes back to Player 1, who turns over another card and tries to make the target total.

5. Play ends when all target totals from 6 to 12 have been made, or when there are no more cards in the facedown pile. The winner is the player with the most cards.

Target Total	Addition Sentence
6	
7	
8	
9	
10	
11	
12	

Today's Number:

3

Name _____

First, draw a box around the problems that will have even answers. Then solve the problems.

I. $6 + 3 =$ _____   **2.** $7 - 3 =$ _____   **3.** $10 - 3 =$ _____

4. $9 + 3 =$ _____   **5.** $3 + 8 =$ _____   **6.** $15 - 3 =$ _____

7. $5 + 3 =$ _____   **8.** $6 - 3 =$ _____   **9.** $7 + 3 =$ _____

For each clock, tell how many minutes have passed since the hour.

10. _____ minutes   **II.** _____ minutes   **12.** _____ minutes

 DRAW

 WRITE

_____

_____

_____

_____

Today's Number:

4

Name _____

First, draw a box around the problems that will have even answers. Then solve the problems.

I. 3 + 4 = _____   **2.** 5 − 4 = _____   **3.** 6 + 4 = _____

4. 8 + 4 = _____   **5.** 4 + 9 = _____   **6.** 9 − 4 = _____

7. 2 + 4 = _____   **8.** 4 + 4 = _____   **9.** 10 − 4 = _____

Draw four 4-sided shapes. Write the name of each one.

10. _____

Name _____

11. _____

Name _____

12. _____

Name _____

13. _____

Name _____

 DRAW

 WRITE

_____

_____

_____

_____

Place Value Models

Grid Addition

◆ MATERIALS

1 set of Grid Cards cardstock (16 cards), watch or clock with a second hand, paper, pencil

◆ DIRECTIONS

1. Each player makes a recording sheet like the one shown below.

2. Make a grid by arranging the Grid Cards in 4 rows with 4 cards in each row.

3. Player 1 has three minutes to make as many sums to 18 as possible using only adjacent numbers in the grid. For each sum, the number sentence is written on her or his recording sheet. Player 2 watches the clock and says "Time" when three minutes have passed.

4. Players then switch roles.

5. Players compare their recording sheets. Any number sentences appearing on both recording sheets should be crossed out.

6. Players count the remaining number sentences. The player with the most number sentences is the winner.

SUMS	
2	3
4	5
6	7
8	9
10	11
12	13
14	15
16	17
18	

Today's Number:

5

Name_____

First, draw a box around the problems that will have even answers. Then solve the problems.

1. $5 + 5 =$ _____   **2.** $9 - 5 =$ _____   **3.** $8 + 5 =$ _____

4. $5 + 3 =$ _____   **5.** $15 - 5 =$ _____   **6.** $5 + 7 =$ _____

7. $18 - 5 =$ _____   **8.** $5 + 2 =$ _____   **9.** $7 - 5 =$ _____

10. Circle seven ways to make five cents.

11. Five cents equals  nickel or  pennies.

DRAW

WRITE

_____

_____

_____

_____

Place Value Models

Ones	
Tens	

Weekly Newsletter

Each week your child will be bringing home Make & Take activities that have been made and used in class. These activities will provide you with materials to help your child explore mathematical concepts. For additional hints, definitions, or explanations refer to the *Math to Learn** handbook pages listed below each activity title.

This week your child made Fast Fact Cards in school. Play **Fast Facts Match-Up** with your child. Your child has learned how to play this in school, and should be able to teach it to you.

FAST FACTS MATCH-UP

Adding Doubles: 62
Doubles Plus 1: 63

1. Shuffle the Fast Fact Cards and the 2–19 Number Cards separately. Spread them out facedown in two different areas on the table.

2. Player 1 turns over a Fast Fact Card and a Number Card. If the sum shown on the Fast Fact Card matches the total shown on the Number Card, the player takes both cards. If they do not match, both cards are turned facedown and returned to the table.

3. Player 2 turns over a Fast Fact Card and a Number Card and plays in the same way as described above.

4. Players alternate turns until all the cards have been matched. The player with the most cards at the end is the winner.

Here are some other ways you can use the materials your child has brought home.

• Use the Number Cards as flashcards. Hold a card up, and let your child show you the Fast Fact Card that matches it.

• Cover one half of a Fast Fact Card. Tell your child what the total should be, and have him or her tell you the part that is covered.

Your child has been learning about place value this week. Use the **Place Value Models** materials to reinforce the learning that has begun.

PLACE VALUE MODELS

Tens and Ones: 12–15

1. Explain that you will be calling out numbers that your child is to create on the Place Value Mat with the Place Value Pieces. You can use any number up to 99. For example, if you say "39," your child should place 3 tens strips in the tens place and 9 ones squares in the ones place of the Place Value Mat.

2. After your child has made the number on the mat, ask him or her to look at the mat and read the number represented there. For example, 4 ten strips and 8 ones squares might be read as "4 tens and 8 ones makes 48."

3. As your child gains confidence, have him or her call out some numbers for you to create. Your child can use her or his knowledge to check your work.

Have fun, and enjoy the time with your child!

*Math to Learn is a mathematics handbook published by Great Source Education Group. For information on ordering *Math to Learn* call 800-289-4490 or visit www.greatsource.com.

First, draw a triangle around the problems that will have odd answers. Then solve the problems.

1. $6 + 1 =$ _____   **2.** $5 + 6 =$ _____   **3.** $14 - 6 =$ _____

4. $18 - 6 =$ _____   **5.** $9 - 6 =$ _____   **6.** $6 + 7 =$ _____

7. $9 + 6 =$ _____   **8.** $10 + 6 =$ _____   **9.** $10 - 6 =$ _____

Use the graph below to answer questions 10–12.

Favorite ice cream flavors of children in Mrs. Palmer's class										
Vanilla	X	X	X	X	X	X	X			
Chocolate	X	X	X	X	X	X	X	X		
Strawberry										

10. How many children picked chocolate as their favorite flavor? _____

11. There are 20 children in Mrs. Palmer's class. How many like strawberry best? _____

12. Fill in that number of **X**s on the graph.

 DRAW

 WRITE

_____

_____

_____

_____

How Many Inches?

TAB

Yardstick Strips

TAB

MAKE & TAKE

Yardstick Strips   TAB

Name _____

How Many Inches?

Things I want to measure	Estimate	Actual Measurement
1.		
2.		
3.		
4.		
5.		
6.		
7.		

MAKE & TAKE

First, draw a triangle around the problems that will have odd answers. Then solve the problems.

1. $8 + 7 =$ _____

2. $8 - 5 =$ _____

3. $8 - 7 =$ _____

4. $10 + 8 =$ _____

5. $9 - 8 =$ _____

6. $8 + 8 =$ _____

7. $8 + 3 =$ _____

8. $10 - 8 =$ _____

9. $8 + 6 =$ _____

10. $8 - 1 =$ _____

For each pattern, draw the missing shape.

11.

12.

DRAW

WRITE

Say the Number Fast

Say the Number Fast

Get the Total to 18

◆ MATERIALS

2 sets of Ten Grid Cards cardstock (40 cards)

◆ DIRECTIONS

1. Make a recording sheet like the one shown below. Shuffle the cards and place them facedown on the table.

2. The object is to add two or more cards to make each target total in order from 6 to 18. Player 1 turns over two cards. If the two cards make the target total, the player states the addition sentence, writes the number sentence on the recording sheet, and takes the cards. Player 2 then turns over two more cards and tries to make the next higher target total.

3. If the two cards do not make the target total, Player 2 turns over the next card from the facedown pile and tries to make the target total. Using more than two cards is acceptable. If the total can be made, Player 2 states the number sentence, writes it on the recording sheet, and takes the cards.

4. If the cards do not make the target total, play passes back to Player 1, who turns over another card and tries to make the target total.

5. Play ends when all target totals from 6 to 18 have been made, or when there are no more cards in the facedown pile.

6. The winner is the player with the most cards.

Target Total	Addition Sentence	Target Total	Addition Sentence
6		13	
7		14	
8		15	
9		16	
10		17	
11		18	
12			

Today's Number: 9

Name_____

First, draw a triangle around the problems that will have odd answers. Then solve the problems.

1. $8 + 9 =$ _____ 2. $9 - 6 =$ _____ 3. $9 - 1 =$ _____

4. $9 + 2 =$ _____ 5. $10 + 9 =$ _____ 6. $9 + 9 =$ _____

7. $9 + 7 =$ _____ 8. $9 - 8 =$ _____ 9. $9 + 6 =$ _____

Add the values of the coins.

10.   = _____

11.   = _____

12.   = _____

13.   = _____

 DRAW    WRITE

_____

_____

_____

_____

PRACTICE

Today's Number:
10

Name _____

First, draw a triangle around the problems that
will have odd answers. Then solve the problems.

1. $10 - 7 =$ _____   **2.** $5 + 10 =$ _____   **3.** $18 - 10 =$ _____

4. $10 + 2 =$ _____   **5.** $10 + 9 =$ _____   **6.** $10 + 6 =$ _____

7. $10 - 1 =$ _____   **8.** $10 - 8 =$ _____   **9.** $10 - 5 =$ _____

Circle groups of ten. Write the number of tens
and ones. Then write the numeral.

10. 〤〤 〤〤
〤〤 〤〤
///

11. 〤〤 〤〤
〤〤 〤〤
〤〤 〤〤
〤〤 〤〤
〤〤 /

12. 〤〤 〤〤
〤〤 〤〤
〤〤 〤〤
〤〤 〤〤
〤〤 〤〤
〤〤 ///

 DRAW

 WRITE

_____

_____

_____

_____

Weekly Newsletter

Each week your child will be bringing home Make & Take activities that have been made and used in class. These activities will provide you with materials to help your child explore mathematical concepts. For additional hints, definitions, or explanations refer to the *Math to Learn* handbook pages listed below each activity title.

This week, your child made a yardstick in school. We have been working to make sure that children know how to use a yardstick as a measuring tool. Here is an activity you can do with your child.

HOW MANY INCHES?

Estimate in Inches: 210
Measure in Inches: 211

1. Take a look at the Recording Sheet your child used in school for this activity. Make a similar list on a separate piece of paper to use as a recording sheet at home.

2. Have your child take the yardstick he or she has made and use it as a reference to choose seven objects around the house that he or she thinks are shorter than the yardstick. Your child should write the names of the objects on his or her recording sheet.

3. Then have your child estimate the length of each of the seven objects. The estimate should also be written on the recording sheet.

4. Then your child should use the yardstick to measure the objects he or she has chosen. The actual measurements should be written on the recording sheet.

Watch as your child measures the objects. Is your child using the yardstick properly and measuring from one end of each object to the other, starting at the beginning of the yardstick?

Your child also made 10 + Fact Cards this week that are used to play **Say the Number Fast**.

SAY THE NUMBER FAST

Ten Frames: 4–5
Numbers 10–19: 6–7

1. Shuffle the 10 + Fact Cards and place them facedown on the table.

2. One player turns over the top card and places it where both players can see it. The first player to say the sum for the 10 + fact shown on the card gets the card. The number sentence for each correct solution should be written on a piece of paper.

3. The other player turns over the next card and play continues in the same way. The first player to state the sum shown on each 10 + Fact Card gets the card.

4. If a player does not agree with the sum stated, he or she can challenge the player who made the statement. If the challenge is correct, the card goes to the player who made the challenge.

5. Play continues until all the 10 + Fact Cards have been used. The player with the most cards wins the game.

As a variation, the cards can be used as subtraction problems, with the smaller amount being subtracted from 10. The first player to say the difference gets the card. The number sentences should be written on a separate piece of paper.

Enjoy using these materials with your child. We hope these activities help you see what your child is learning in school.

PRACTICE

Today's Number: 11

Name _____

Add or subtract. Draw a circle around the problems
that are Doubles or Doubles +1.

1. 11 + 9 = _____ **2.** 10 + 9 = _____ **3.** 11 − 8 = _____

4. 7 + 11 = _____ **5.** 11 + 11 = _____ **6.** 8 + 9 = _____

Write the numbers for the place value materials shown.

7.

___ Tens + ___ Ones = _____

8.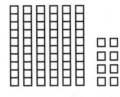

___ Tens + ___ Ones = _____

9.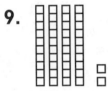

___ Tens + ___ Ones = _____

10.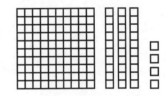

___ Hundreds + ___ Tens +

___ Ones = _____

 DRAW

 WRITE

_____

_____

_____

_____

9+ and 8+ Fast Facts

Double Ten Frames

Guess My Number

♦ MATERIALS

1 set of Ten Grid Cards cardstock (20 cards)

♦ DIRECTIONS

1. Organize groups of four children into two pairs each.

2. Shuffle the cards and place them facedown in a pile on the table.

3. A player from one pair draws the top card from the pile. He or she looks at the number on the card but does not show it to his or her partner. The object of the game is to provide good mathematical clues so that the partner can identify the hidden number easily.

4. The player with the card then gives up to three clues about the number to his or her partner. If the partner correctly identifies the number, the pair keeps the card. If the partner cannot identify the number from the clues, the card is discarded.

5. Play alternates between pairs until all the cards in the pile are used.

6. The pair with more cards is the winner.

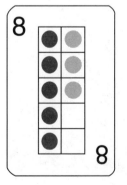

It's an even number. It's greater than 7. If you add 2, you get 10.

Add or subtract. Draw a circle around the problems that are Doubles or Doubles +1.

1. 12 + 8 = _____   **2.** 12 − 6 = _____   **3.** 12 + 13 = _____

4. 12 + 9 = _____   **5.** 24 − 12 = _____   **6.** 7 + 5 = _____

7. 12 + 10 + 5 = _____   **8.** 6 + 7 = _____

This is a fact family for 5, 7, and 12:

5 + 7 = 12, 7 + 5 = 12, 12 − 7 = 5, 12 − 5 = 7

Complete the fact families for each set of numbers.

9. 12 − 9 = 3   _____

10. 8 + 4 = 12   _____

11. 2 + 10 = 12   _____

12. 6 + 6 = 12   _____

DRAW   WRITE

_____

_____

_____

_____

Add or subtract. Draw a circle around the problems that are Doubles or Doubles +1.

1. $13 - 6 =$ _____ 2. $13 + 8 =$ _____ 3. $9 + 8 =$ _____

4. $13 - 9 =$ _____ 5. $10 + 13 =$ _____ 6. $13 + 13 =$ _____

7. $23 + 9 =$ _____ 8. $23 + 4 =$ _____ 9. $15 - 7 =$ _____

Use the stars to answer questions 10–13.

10. Draw a circle around the 1st star.

11. Draw a triangle around the 3rd star.

12. Draw a dot above the 10th star.

13. Draw a box around the 12th star.

Circle the true statement.

14. $13 = 9 + 3$ $13 < 10$ $13 > 17$ $13 > 9$

 DRAW    WRITE

_____

_____

_____

_____

MAKE & TAKE

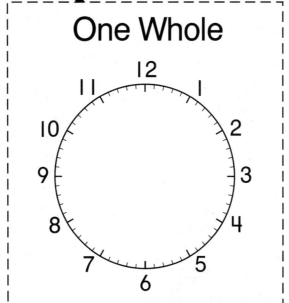

One Whole

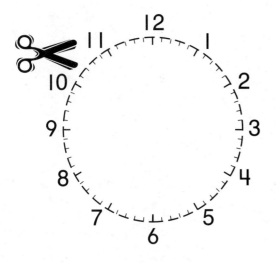

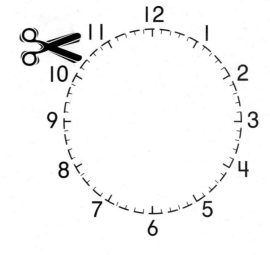

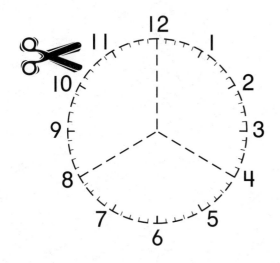

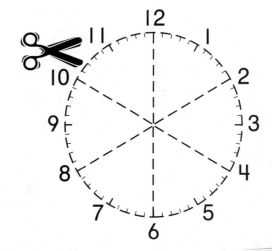

Grid Addition and Subtraction

◆ MATERIALS

1 set of Grid Cards (16 cards), watch or clock
with a second hand, paper, pencil

◆ DIRECTIONS

1. Each player makes a recording sheet like the one shown
   below.

2. Make a grid by arranging the Grid Cards in 4 rows with 4
   cards in each row.

3. Players choose a target number between 2 and 18. Each
   player writes the target number in a box on the recording sheet.

4. Player 1 has three minutes to make as many addition and
   subtraction facts as possible for the target number using
   only adjacent numbers in the grid. Each number sentence is
   written on the recording sheet. Player 2 watches the clock
   and says "Time" when three minutes have passed. Players
   then switch roles.

5. After this first round, players compare the number sentences
   they have written and cross out any that are the same.

6. To continue, pick up the cards, shuffle them, and make a
   new grid. Players select a new target number. Play
   continues as it did in the first round.

7. After 5 rounds, players count the remaining number
   sentences on their recording sheets. The player with the
   most number sentences is the winner.

Name _____		
Target Number		**Number Sentences**
Round 1		
Round 2		
Round 3		
Round 4		
Round 5		

Name _____

Add or subtract. Draw a circle around the problems that are Doubles or Doubles +1.

1. $14 - 9 =$ _____ 2. $14 + 10 =$ _____ 3. $7 + 7 =$ _____

4. $14 + 15 =$ _____ 5. $28 - 14 =$ _____ 6. $7 + 8 =$ _____

7. $14 - 8 =$ _____ 8. $20 - 14 =$ _____ 9. $14 + 9 =$ _____

Use the calendar to answer questions 10–12.

10. What month is it? _____

11. If today is June 14, what date will it be tomorrow? _____

12. What date will it be on the third Saturday of the month? _____

			JUNE			
Sun.	Mon.	Tues.	Wed.	Thur.	Fri.	Sat.
	1	2	3	4	5	6
7	8	9	10	11	12	13
14						

 DRAW

 WRITE

_____

_____

_____

_____

Add or subtract. Draw a circle around the problems that are Doubles or Doubles +1.

1. 15 + 10 = _____   **2.** 5 + 6 = _____   **3.** 15 − 8 = _____

4. 24 − 15 = _____   **5.** 15 + 8 = _____   **6.** 15 + 15 = _____

7. 5 + 10 + 9 = _____   **8.** 20 + 15 = _____

Fill in the blanks in each pattern.

9. 4, 8, 12, _____, 20, _____, 28, 32, _____

10. 35, 40, 45, 50, _____, 60, 65, _____, 75, _____, 85

11. 30, 40, 50, _____, 70, _____, 90, _____

12. Describe the pattern in question 11. _____

_____

 DRAW    WRITE

_____

_____

_____

_____

Weekly Newsletter

Each week your child will be bringing home Make & Take activities that have been made and used in class. These activities will provide you with materials to help your child explore mathematical concepts. For additional hints, definitions, or explanations refer to the *Math to Learn* handbook pages listed below each activity title.

This week, your child made **9+ and 8+ Fast Fact** cards. In class, we have been discussing how to use "Fast Tens" as a strategy to solve the 9+ and 8+ problems. Ask your child to explain this approach to you.

9+ AND 8+ FAST FACTS

Make a Ten to Add: 64
Add to 9: 65

1. Both you and your child will need a piece of paper and a pencil.

2. Place the Fast Fact Cards facedown in a stack on the table.

3. The first player turns the top card over and states the number sentence for the addition fact shown on that card. Then the second player does the same. Both players write the two sums on their recording sheets.

4. The player with the higher sum makes a comparison of the two sums, for example, "17 is 3 more than 14," and writes the addition fact and the comparison on the paper. That player keeps both cards.

5. If the sums of the faceup cards are equal, players turn over the next cards from the facedown stack and continue to play.

6. Play continues until there are no cards left to turn over. The player with more sums and comparisons written on the paper is the winner.

If you think your child may need some more practice with these addition facts, use the cards as flash cards. Have you child read the fact shown on the card and give you the sum.

Your child also made **Clock Fractions** this week to help him or her understand how parts relate to wholes. Clocks provide an easy way to recognize fractions in our daily lives.

CLOCK FRACTIONS

Tell Time: 182–185
Fraction of a Whole: 43–47

• See how many ways your child can make one whole clock with the different fraction pieces.

• Fill in the whole clock leaving out one fraction piece. See if your child can correctly identify which piece will complete the clock.

• Have your child practice writing the fraction names of the pieces represented by the Clock Fractions.

If you happen to have a pizza this week, remember to point out the fractional parts made by each piece!

Enjoy the time with your child, and thank you for helping to strengthen the mathematical tie between home and school.

In which problems can you make a Fast Ten?
Solve only those problems after rewriting them
as Fast Ten number sentences.

1. $8 + 9 =$ _____

2. $16 + 9 =$ _____

3. $16 + 3 =$ _____

4. $16 + 8 =$ _____

Circle the groups of coins whose value is 40¢.

5.

6.

7.

8.

9.

10.

 DRAW

 WRITE

_____

_____

_____

_____

Hundred Chart Puzzle

1	2	3	4	5	6	7	8	9	10
11	12	13	14	15	16	17	18	19	20
21	22	23	24	25	26	27	28	29	30
31	32	33	34	35	36	37	38	39	40
41	42	43	44	45	46	47	48	49	50
51	52	53	54	55	56	57	58	59	60
61	62	63	64	65	66	67	68	69	70
71	72	73	74	75	76	77	78	79	80
81	82	83	84	85	86	87	88	89	90
91	92	93	94	95	96	97	98	99	100

Let's Go Fast Tens!

◆ MATERIALS

One 4–9 number cube; I set of Ten Frames cardstock (10 Ten Frames); 100 beans, small construction paper squares, or other counters

◆ DIRECTIONS

1. Each player uses 5 Ten Frames. The goal is to be the first player to fill all 5 Ten Frames with exactly 50 counters.

2. The first player rolls the number cube. She or he places that number of counters on the first of her or his Ten Frames.

3. The second player rolls the number cube and places that number of counters on his or her Ten Frame.

4. The first player states the total shown on her or his Ten Frames, and then rolls the number cube. If a Fast Ten can be made with the counters to be added, the player tells how it can be done. For example, "I have 24 and I rolled an 8. 24 plus 6 is 30, and 2 more is 32." On the other hand, if a Fast Ten is not possible, the player still places the appropriate number of counters on his or her Ten Frame and states that a Fast Ten cannot be made.

5. The second player repeats the same steps.

6. Play alternates back and forth until one of the players has filled the Ten Frames with exactly 50 counters. That player is the winner.

Today's Number: **17**

Name _____

In which problems can you make a Fast Ten?
Solve only those problems after rewriting them
as Fast Ten number sentences.

1. 17 + 9 = _____

2. 17 + 2 = _____

3. 17 + 2 + 3 = _____

4. 17 + 7 = _____

5. 17 + 1 = _____

6. 17 + 6 = _____

Circle the shapes that have one half shaded.

7.   **8.**   **9.**   **10.**   **11.**

DRAW

WRITE

_____

_____

_____

_____

In which problems can you make a Fast Ten?
Solve only those problems after rewriting them
as Fast Ten number sentences.

1. $18 + 4 =$ _____

2. $18 + 9 =$ _____

3. $18 + 3 =$ _____

4. $18 + 1 =$ _____

Solve each problem and show your work.

5. Marcy has $18. Sabrina has $9.
   What is the difference between the two amounts? _____

6. It takes Ben 20 minutes to read
   5 pages in his book. How many
   minutes does it take him to read 1 page? _____

 DRAW

 WRITE

_____

_____

_____

_____

Sharing Quarters

Who Has the Least?

MATERIALS

2 sets of Ten Grid Cards cardstock (40 cards)

DIRECTIONS

1. Shuffle the Ten Grid Cards and place them facedown in a stack between the two players.

2. Each player turns over a card from the stack. The player whose number is lower makes a comparison statement about the two numbers. For example, "4 is less than 8." The same player then identifies the difference between the two numbers, "The difference is 4."

3. If the comparison sentence is correct and the difference is correctly identified, the player keeps both cards. If the second player thinks an error has been made, she or he can challenge the first player to prove his or her statements. If an error has been made, the player who made the challenge takes both cards. If both cards drawn are equal, each player keeps his or her card.

The difference is four.

4. The game ends when all cards have been used. The player with more cards is the winner.

In which problems can you make a Fast Ten?
Solve only those problems after rewriting them
as Fast Ten number sentences.

1. $19 + 3 =$ _____

2. $19 - 10 =$ _____

3. $19 + 8 =$ _____

4. $19 + 9 =$ _____

5. $19 + 5 =$ _____

For each number, draw a triangle around the digit
in the ones place. Then circle the number with the
greatest digit in the ones place.

6. 526   7. 920   8. 834   9. 4521

 DRAW    WRITE

_____

_____

_____

_____

Today's Number:
20

Name _____

Solve only the problems whose answers are even numbers.

1. 20 + 4 = _____   **2.** 20 − 2 = _____   **3.** 20 + 9 = _____

4. 20 + 8 = _____   **5.** 20 + 10 = _____   **6.** 20 − 5 = _____

7. 20 − 6 = _____   **8.** 20 − 4 = _____   **9.** 20 + 12 = _____

Write each group of numbers in order from least to greatest.

10. 10, 1, 8, 7, 5 _____

11. 58, 53, 59, 51, 57 _____

12. 123, 129, 120, 124, 127 _____

13. 586, 581, 590, 582, 584 _____

14. 109, 227, 8, 32, 223 _____

DRAW   WRITE

_____

_____

_____

_____

Weekly Newsletter

Each week your child will be bringing home Make & Take activities that have been made and used in class. These activities will provide you with materials to help your child explore mathematical concepts. For additional hints, definitions, or explanations refer to the *Math to Learn* handbook pages listed below each activity title.

This week, your child made a **Hundred Chart Puzzle**. This puzzle is designed to help your child see the important patterns within our number system. The puzzle also gives your child an opportunity to develop his or her spatial awareness. Here are some activities you can do with the puzzle.

HUNDRED CHART PUZZLE

Numbers to 99: 8–15
Just Before and Just After: 33
Odd and Even Numbers: 36–37
Mental Addition: 114-115

1. Have your child let <u>you</u> try to put the puzzle pieces together! Your child can help you if you need hints!

2. Hide a piece of the puzzle before your child puts the puzzle together. When all the available pieces are put together, add the missing piece only after your child names the numbers that are missing from the chart.

3. Once the puzzle is together, have your child show you the number patterns for counting by tens, fives, and twos on the puzzle.

Your child also made a **Sharing Quarters** activity this week. Here are some ways you can use it together.

SHARING QUARTERS

Counting Quarters: 168
Division: 108–111

1. Ask your child to arrange the Quarter Cards into two equal groups. How many

quarters would each of you have? (12) How much money would each of you have? ($3)

2. Have your child make a statement about the sharing. For example, 24 quarters shared equally between 2 people is 12 quarters for each person. See if he or she can express the same statement using a "groups of" model. For example, 2 groups of 12 is 24.

3. Repeat the same steps, asking your child to arrange the quarters into three, four, six, and eight equal groups. For each arrangement, have her or him make a "sharing equally" and a "groups of" statement. He or she should also tell you the value of the quarters in each group.

4. Each step can also be checked with addition, so your child can see more than one way to check his or her work. For example, 24 quarters shared equally in 6 groups is 4 in each group; 6 groups of 4 is 24; or 4 added 6 times is 24.

5. Ask your child to arrange the quarters as equally as possible into five, seven, and nine groups. In each case, ask how many quarters are left over. You can also ask how many more quarters are needed so there are no leftovers.

While doing this activity with your child, check to see that there is understanding of sharing in equal groups. This concept becomes important when your child begins to divide. Also check that your child can make the "groups of" statements easily. This is an early way to understand the concept of multiplication.

Enjoy this learning and reviewing time with your child.

First, draw a box around the problem that will have the greatest answer. Then solve the problems.

1. $21 + 19 =$ _____ 2. $38 - 21 =$ _____ 3. $21 + 27 =$ _____

4. $56 + 21 =$ _____ 5. $47 + 21 =$ _____ 6. $21 - 10 =$ _____

7. $34 - 21 =$ _____ 8. $2 \times 5 =$ _____ 9. $3 \times 4 =$ _____

Draw a circle around any shapes that are cylinders.
Draw a star next to any shapes that are rectangular prisms.

 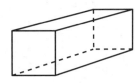 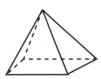

 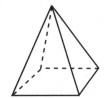

DRAW

WRITE

_____

_____

_____

_____

Scavenger Hunt

1. Find an object that is the shape of a rectangular prism.

   What object did you find? _____

2. How many desks are in the classroom? _____

   Is that an odd or an even number? _____

3. Find a two-digit number written somewhere.

   What number did you find? _____

   Where did you find it? _____

4. Find something that is equal to the length of a ruler.

   What object did you find? _____

5. What time is it right now? _____

6. What is today's date? _____

7. Find a penny. What is the year on the penny? _____

8. Write the number address of your house or the school. _____

   Add the digits together. What is the sum? _____

   Double that number. What do you get? _____

9. What is your school room number? _____

10. What day of the month were you born? _____

    If you add 5 to that number, what number do you get? _____

Make 50 Cents

◆ MATERIALS

One 1–6 number cube, 1 set of Coin Cards I cardstock (20 cards) and 1 set of Coin Cards II cardstock (20 cards) or real coins

◆ DIRECTIONS

1. Player 1 rolls the number cube and takes that amount in cents. For example, if a 3 is rolled, the player takes 3 cents. If the player rolls a 6, he or she may take 1 nickel and 1 penny or 6 pennies.

2. Whenever possible, coins are traded for the next higher denomination.

3. Player 2 repeats the same steps, making sure to trade the coins whenever possible.

4. The player who collects 5 dimes (50 cents) first is the winner.

> I get 4 cents.
> I already have 17 cents.
> I need to trade 5 pennies
> and a nickel for a dime.
> Now I have 21 cents.

First, draw a box around the problem that will have
the greatest answer. Then solve the problems.

1. 29 + 22 = _____   **2.** 18 + 22 = _____   **3.** 45 − 22 = _____

4. 52 + 22 = _____   **5.** 12 + 22 = _____   **6.** 3 × 2 + 10 = _____

7. 22 + 30 + 23 = _____   **8.** 22 − 9 − 5 = _____

9. 2 × 4 = _____   **10.** 54 − 22 − 11 = _____

In these Addition Triangles, the sum is in the box at
the top of the triangle. The numbers in the boxes at
the bottom of the triangle are added to make the sum.
For each problem, write the missing number in the box.

11. 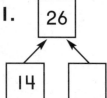   **12.** 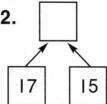   **13.** 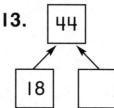   **14.**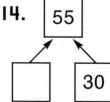

 DRAW    WRITE

First, draw a box around the problem that will have the greatest answer. Then solve the problems.

1. $23 + 10 + 4 =$ _____   2. $23 + 28 =$ _____

3. $30 - 23 =$ _____   4. $49 + 23 =$ _____

5. $23 + 10 + 13 =$ _____   6. $56 + 23 =$ _____

7. $33 + 23 =$ _____   8. $65 - 23 =$ _____

9. $2 \times 5 =$ _____   10. $44 - 23 - 4 =$ _____

For each problem, draw a circle around one group of numbers to match the sum.

Example: Sum = 20   9 (4 6 5 5) 8

11. **Sum = 23** 3 7 8 5 9 2   12. **Sum = 18** 5 7 1 8 8 1

13. **Sum = 25** 5 9 7 2 7 3   14. **Sum = 29** 8 3 9 2 6 1

 **DRAW**    **WRITE**

_____

_____

_____

_____

Rounding Tape

ROUNDING TAPE GAME BOARD

0 Start

1 2 3 4 5 6 7 8 9 10 11 12 13 14 15 16 17 18 19 20 21 22 23 24 25 26 27 28 29 30 31 32 33 34 35 36 37 38 39 40 41 42 43 44 45 46 47 48 49 50 51 52 53 54 55 56 57 58 59 60 61 62 63 64 65 66 67 68 69 70 71 72 73 74 75 76 77 78 79 80 81 82 83 84 85 86 87 88 89 90 91 92 93 94 95 96 97 98 99 100

Guess My Sum

◆ MATERIALS

2 sets of Ten Grid Cards cardstock (40 cards)

◆ DIRECTIONS

1. Organize groups of four children into two pairs each.

2. Shuffle the cards and place them facedown in a pile on the table.

3. A player from one pair draws the top two cards from the pile. He or she looks at the numbers on the cards but does not show them to his or her partner. The object of the game is to provide good mathematical clues so that the partner can identify the hidden sum easily.

4. The player with the cards then gives up to three clues about the sum of the two numbers to his or her partner. If the partner correctly identifies the sum, the pair keeps the cards. If the partner cannot identify the sum from the clues, the cards are discarded.

5. Play alternates between pairs until all the cards in the pile are used.

6. The pair with more cards is the winner.

Name_____

First, draw a box around the problem that will have the greatest answer. Then solve the problems.

1. $24 + 28 =$ _____

2. $47 + 24 =$ _____

3. $32 - 24 =$ _____

4. $24 + 12 + 5 =$ _____

5. $30 - 24 =$ _____

6. $35 + 24 =$ _____

7. $24 - 15 =$ _____

8. $7 + 2 + 10 =$ _____

9. $3 \times 5 =$ _____

10. $3 + 2 + 24 =$ _____

For each problem, write the missing numbers in the Hundred Chart puzzle pieces.

Example:

21		
31	**32**	33
	42	**43**
		53

11.

68		70
88		
		100

12.

	26	
		38
47		49

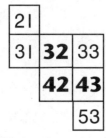

DRAW

WRITE

_____

_____

_____

_____

Name _____

First, draw a box around the problem that will have the greatest answer. Then solve the problems.

1. 25 + 19 = _____   2. 38 + 25 = _____

3. 44 + 25 = _____   4. 25 + 10 + 19 = _____

5. 40 − 25 − 10 = _____   6. 25 + 16 = _____

7. 2 + 10 + 5 = _____   8. 5 × 5 = _____

Circle the coins you would use to buy each item.

9.

10.

 DRAW    WRITE

_____

_____

_____

_____

Weekly Newsletter

Each week your child will be bringing home Make & Take activities that have been made and used in class. These activities will provide you with materials to help your child explore mathematical concepts. For additional hints, definitions, or explanations refer to the *Math to Learn* handbook pages listed below each activity title.

This week, your child went on a **Scavenger Hunt** in our classroom. The object was to find examples of how numbers are used in our world. Ask your child to tell you what kind of things he or she found at school.

SCAVENGER HUNT

Solid Figures: 204–205
Odd and Even Numbers: 36–37
Time to the Minute: 186
Calendar: 190–191

We worked together as a class to write a list of things to look for at home. Take a look at the list your child has brought home. Complete the Scavenger Hunt with your child and write down the objects that were found or used. In addition, you can:

- Create your own Home Scavenger Hunt. You may have other ideas for objects or number examples that can be found in your home.

- If you happen to be heading for the grocery store, make a special list of things your child can find there.

This is a great opportunity for your child to investigate numbers in her or his environment.

Your child also made and learned to play a **Rounding Tape** game this week. This is an opportunity for your child to investigate rounding numbers to the nearest ten. Ask your child to explain what the colors on the game board mean. Then play the game together. You will need to find two small objects to use as game markers and a 1–6 number cube. If that is not available, make some paper squares with the numbers 1–6 written on them. You can draw the paper squares out of a paper bag for each turn.

ROUNDING TAPE

Rounding: 40–41

1. Players take turns rolling the number cube and moving their game markers ahead by that amount on the game board.

2. Upon landing on a numbered space, each player must round that number to the nearest ten and move her or his game marker to the rounded number. For example, if a player lands on a number ending in 1 through 4, he or she rounds down and moves the marker backward to the nearest ten. Numbers ending in 5 through 9 mean that the player moves the game marker forward to the nearest ten. If a player lands on a number ending in a zero, the game marker stays there.

3. On each turn, the player must state the rounding process being used to determine where his or her game marker will be placed. For example, "I landed on 26. That number rounds up to 30, so I get to move my marker ahead to 30."

4. The first player to reach 100 is the winner.

You may also want to ask your child to round numbers you supply. Note how quickly your child can round the numbers.

Enjoy the math time with your child!

Solve only the problems in which you will have to regroup.

1. 26 + 36 = _____ **2.** 26 + 13 = _____ **3.** 72 − 26 = _____

4. 45 + 26 = _____ **5.** 39 + 26 = _____ **6.** 36 − 26 = _____

7. 29 + 26 = _____ **8.** 108 + 26 = _____ **9.** 29 − 26 = _____

For problems 10–13, the operation sign and number in the first box tell you what to do to find the missing numbers.

Example: | +5 | | 7 | → | 12 | → | 17 | → | 22 |

10. | −4 | | 20 | → | 16 | → | ☐ | → | ☐ | → | ☐ |

11. | +3 | | 7 | → | 10 | → | ☐ | → | ☐ | → | ☐ |

12. | +7 | | 1 | → | 8 | → | ☐ | → | ☐ | → | ☐ |

13. | −10 | | 59 | → | ☐ | → | ☐ | → | ☐ | → | ☐ |

DRAW  WRITE

_____

_____

_____

_____

Ordinal Parking

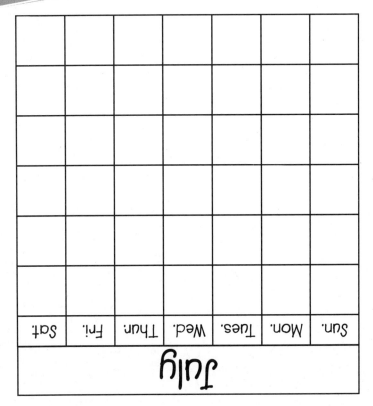

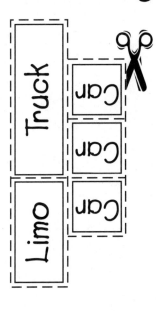

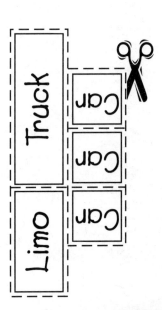

July

Sun.	Mon.	Tues.	Wed.	Thur.	Fri.	Sat.

Two-Digit Fast Tens

◆ MATERIALS

One 1–6 number cube, one 4–9 number cube, 10 Counters cardstock, Place Value Materials cardstock

◆ DIRECTIONS

1. Player 1 rolls the number cubes and uses the numbers to make the lowest two-digit number possible. For example, with a 4 and a 5, the player can make 45 or 54. The lowest number possible is 45.

2. Player 1 then displays that two-digit number using the Place Value Materials.

3. Player 2 then rolls the number cubes, makes the lowest two-digit number possible, and displays that number using the Place Value Materials.

4. Player 1 rolls the number cubes again, makes the lowest possible two-digit number, and displays the number using the Place Value Materials. Then that player adds both numbers he or she has made. If a Fast Ten can be made, the player tells how it can be made. For example, "I had 45 and I rolled a 6 and an 8, or 68. I need to add 68 and 45. 68 plus 2 more is 70. That is a Fast Ten. 70 plus 43 is 113." The Place Value Materials should be used to show the addition, with ones traded for tens and tens traded for one hundred whenever possible.

5. Player 2 repeats the same steps.

6. The player with the lower sum wins the round and gets one counter.

7. The first player to win 5 rounds is the winner of the game.

Today's Number:

27

Name _____

Solve only the problems in which you will have to regroup.

1. 27 + 9 = _____ 2. 18 + 27 = _____ 3. 110 + 27 = _____

4. 56 + 27 = _____ 5. 27 − 10 = _____ 6. 45 − 27 = _____

7. 68 + 27 = _____ 8. 32 + 27 = _____ 9. 44 + 27 = _____

For problems 10–13, write the amount of change you would receive from each purchase.

You buy:	You give the clerk:	Your change is:
10. a toy for 30 cents	2 quarters	_____
11. a pencil for 27 cents	1 quarter and 1 dime	_____
12. a book for 55 cents	1 dollar	_____
13. a piece of pizza for 75 cents	8 dimes	_____

 DRAW

 WRITE

_____

_____

_____

_____

Today's Number: 28

Name _____

Solve only the problems in which you will have to regroup.

1. 28 + 18 = _____   2. 45 − 28 = _____

3. 28 − 10 = _____   4. 106 + 28 = _____

5. 30 + 28 = _____   6. 3 + 7 + 6 + 28 = _____

7. 35 + 28 = _____   8. 28 + 20 = _____

9. 28 + 28 = _____   10. 73 − 28 = _____

Use the digits 3, 5, 7, and 8 to solve problems 11−14.

11. Make an odd two-digit number. _____

12. Make an even three-digit number. _____

13. Make a number between 50 and 70. _____

14. Make an odd number greater than 60. _____

 DRAW    WRITE

_____

_____

_____

_____

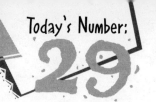
Solve only the problems in which you will have to regroup.

1. 29 + 29 = _____   **2.** 10 + 29 = _____   **3.** 42 + 29 = _____

4. 29 + 51 = _____   **5.** 29 − 12 = _____   **6.** 123 + 29 = _____

7. 2 × 8 + 29 = _____   **8.** 29 + 1 + 4 + 6 = _____

For problems 9–12, match each number with its place value amount.

9. 29

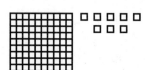

10. 35

11. 108

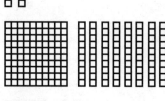

12. 180

 **DRAW**    **WRITE**

_____

_____

_____

_____

Today's Number:
30

Name _____

Solve only the problems in which you will have to regroup.

1. 30 + 10 = _____

2. 30 + 9 + 7 = _____

3. 80 − 30 = _____

4. 45 + 17 + 30 = _____

5. 290 + 30 = _____

6. 6 × 5 = _____

7. 183 + 30 = _____

8. 37 + 18 + 30 = _____

9. 10 + 30 + 4 + 8 = _____

10. Draw circles around groups of numbers whose sum is 30. Use every number in the grid once.

10	9	11	12	5
2	8	14	6	13
20	5	17	18	4
5	6	4	3	4
10	20	15	15	4

 DRAW

 WRITE

_____

_____

_____

_____

Weekly Newsletter

Each week your child will be bringing home Make & Take activities that have been made and used in class. These activities will provide you with materials to help your child explore mathematical concepts. For additional hints, definitions, or explanations refer to the *Math to Learn* handbook pages listed below each activity title.

This week, your child made and learned to play a game called **Ordinal Parking**. This is an opportunity for your child to practice using ordinal words for numbers.

ORDINAL PARKING

Calendar: 190–191
Ordinal Numbers: 35
Use Logical Reasoning: 292–293

1. Players sit across from each other with a game board between them. A large book, notebook, or some other object is placed upright in the middle of the game board to prevent players from seeing the other calendar.

2. Each player uses 1 truck, 1 limo, and 3 car game pieces. Players "park" the game pieces on numbered squares of their calendars. The truck must completely cover 3 numbered squares, the limo must cover 2 squares, and each car must cover 1 square. The vehicles cannot be parked next to each other horizontally (side to side) or vertically (up and down).

3. The object of the game is to be the first player to determine on which calendar squares the other player has "parked" his or her vehicles.

4. Player 1 asks Player 2 if a particular square is covered or empty. The question must be asked using an ordinal word for the calendar date, for example, "Is the fifteenth covered or empty?" If the question is not asked in that form, the questioning player loses the turn and play passes to the other player.

5. Players alternate turns and record information about covered and empty squares on a piece of paper. As more questions are asked it becomes possible to tell where each vehicle is parked. The first player to correctly identify the location of all the other player's vehicles is the winner.

Over the summer we have played math games at school that have given your child an opportunity to use math in an environment that is fun. Our class voted to select our three favorite games to make and take home to play. Have your child explain how each of the games is played. Encourage him or her to share any strategies learned to win the games. Play the games with your child and talk about the math involved. Share any winning strategies you learn with your child.

These games will give you a chance to see your child use math that she or he understands.

If your child remembers other math games from the summer, encourage him or her to try to create the necessary cards or other materials to play the games with you. Playing math games is a wonderful way to help your child learn and use the math skills we have studied this summer.

Enjoy these games with your child. Thank you again for your part in strengthening the connection between learning at school and at home.

Name _____

Choose the best answer for each question.

1. What number do the base ten materials represent?

   ○ 130
   ○ 113
   ○ 103
   ○ 13

2. What number is the same as five hundred sixty?

   50060   560   506   56
     ○   ○   ○   ○

3. What is the value of the 3 in 359?

   ○ 3 ones   ○ 3 hundreds
   ○ 3 tens   ○ 3 thousands

4. Which number has a 5 in the tens place?

   356   635   536   645
    ○   ○   ○   ○

5. What number is 30 more than 248?

   248   251   278   548
    ○   ○   ○   ○

6. Which group of numbers is in order from least to greatest?

   ○ 401, 410, 400, 407
   ○ 410, 407, 401, 400
   ○ 400, 401, 407, 410
   ○ 407, 410, 400, 401

7. Which statement is true?

   ○ 804 < 803
   ○ 810 > 801
   ○ 801 < 800
   ○ 801 = 810

8. Draw an "X" on the twelfth circle.

   ○○○○○○○○○○○○○○○○○○○○○○○○○

9. Which picture shows 3 out of 4 equal parts shaded?

   ○ 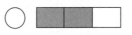   ○

   ○   ○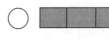

10. What is the missing number in the number pattern?

110, 210, 310, 410, ☐, 610, 710,...

    410   420   510   610
    ○   ○   ○   ○

11. I am a whole number less than 10. When you subtract five from nine, I am the answer. Which number line has a star on me?

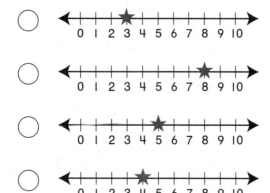

    ○

    ○

    ○

    ○

12. Which is a set of even numbers?

○ 16 18 20   ○ 15 20 21

○ 13 15 19   ○ 16 18 19

13. Which number sentence is in the same family of facts as 8 + 7?

○ 8 − 7 = 1   ○ 15 − 1 = 14

○ 15 + 8 = 23   ○ 15 − 8 = 7

14. About how many units long is the pair of scissors?

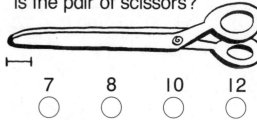

    7   8   10   12
    ○   ○   ○   ○

15. Josh had the following coins in his pocket. How much money did he have?

○ 83¢
○ 80¢
○ 58¢
○ 50¢

16. Katrice and Jerry went to a garage sale where they found a ball on sale for 65¢. Katrice has 4 dimes and Jerry has 6 nickels. Do they have enough money to buy the ball? Why or why not? Show your work.

_____

17. 28 + 45 = _____

_____

18. 96 − 78 = _____

19. 519 + 87 = _____

20.
```
   34
   46
 + 38
```

21. 2 × 8 = _____

22. What time is shown on the clock?

○ 3:55
○ 3:50
○ 4:55
○ 4:00

23. Look at the figures in the box.

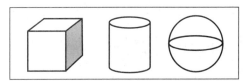

Which figure does NOT belong to this group?

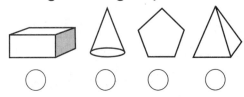

○   ○   ○   ○

24. Which object is shaped like a cube?

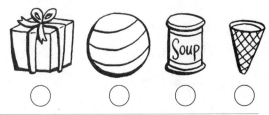

○   ○   ○   ○

25. The table shows the types of pets owned by second-grade students. Which graph matches the facts given in the table?

Kind of Pet	Number of Students
Cat	8
Dog	12
Fish	6
Other	4

○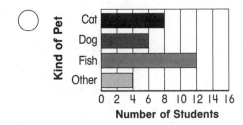

○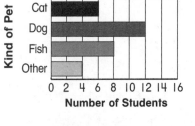

○

○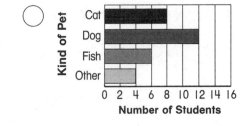

26. What will be the date of the fourth Tuesday on this calendar?

```
              JULY
Sun. Mon. Tues. Wed. Thurs. Fri. Sat.
              1    2    3    4   5
  6   7   8    9   10   11  12
```

○ 13 ○ 15 ○ 22 ○ 29

27. Terry, Anita, Carlos, and Edith ran a race. Terry came in before Carlos. Edith came in behind at least one other person. Anita came in before Terry. Who won the race?

○ Terry
○ Anita
○ Carlos
○ Edith

28. Tomas is reading a book that has 93 pages in it. He has read 45 pages. How many more pages does Tomas have to read to finish the book?

○ 42 ○ 48 ○ 52 ○ 138

29. Peter bought four tickets to the movies. Each ticket cost $3. Which problem can be used to find how much money the four tickets cost?

○ $4 + 3$
○ $4 - 3$
○ 4×3
○ $4 \div 3$

30. Sarah has 6 cookies that she wants to share with her friend. If she shares equally, how many cookies will each girl get?

○ 6 ○ 5 ○ 4 ○ 3

31. Addie has $30. She spent $12 on a shirt and $11 for a pair of shorts. Which method could be used to find how much money she has left?

○ Add $30, $12, and $11.
○ Add $12 and $11 and then subtract $30.
○ Add $12 and $11 and then subtract that amount from $30.
○ Subtract $30, $12, and $11.

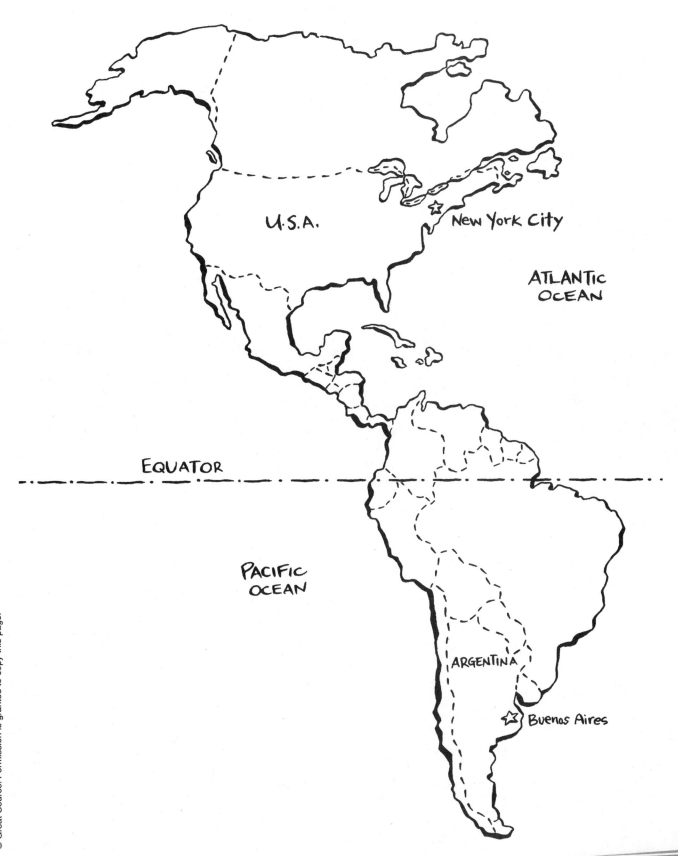

U.S.A.

New York City

ATLANTIC OCEAN

EQUATOR

PACIFIC OCEAN

ARGENTINA

Buenos Aires

July Temperatures (°F)

	New York City	Buenos Aires
Day 1	74°	45°
Day 2	79°	56°
Day 3	75°	55°
Day 4	80°	60°
Day 5	77°	49°

Summer Success: Math

Games to Take Home

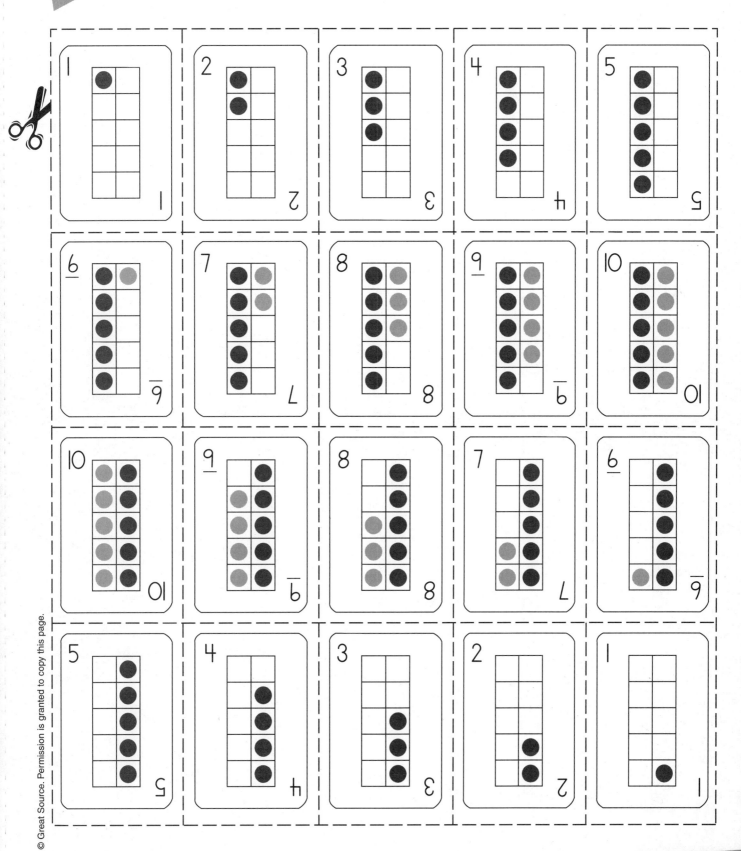

Games to Take Home

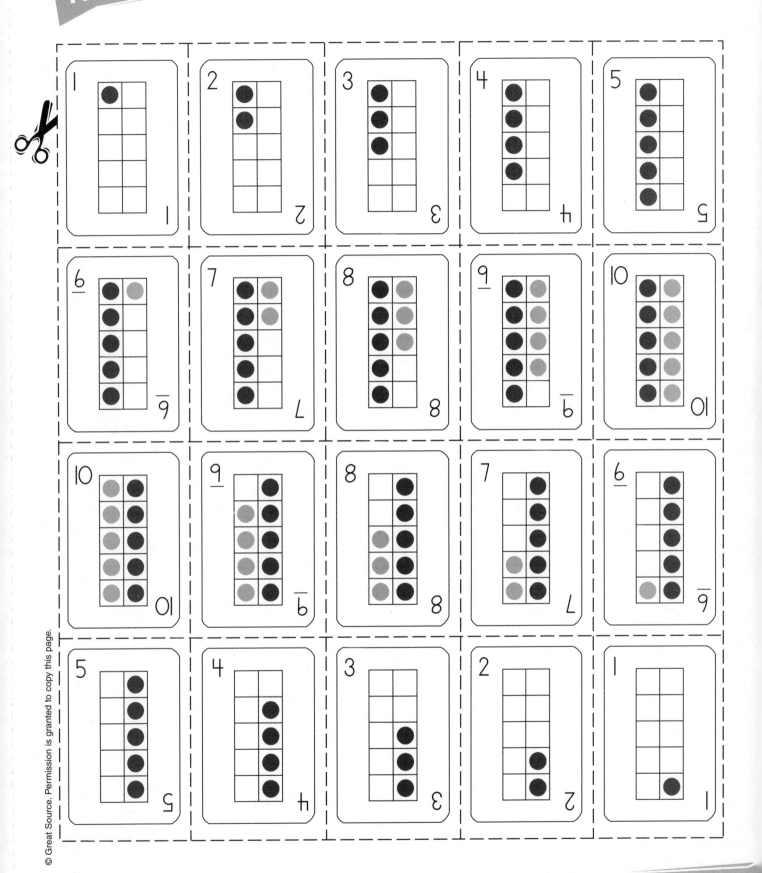

Ten Grid Cards   Grade 2   **105**

Games to Take Home

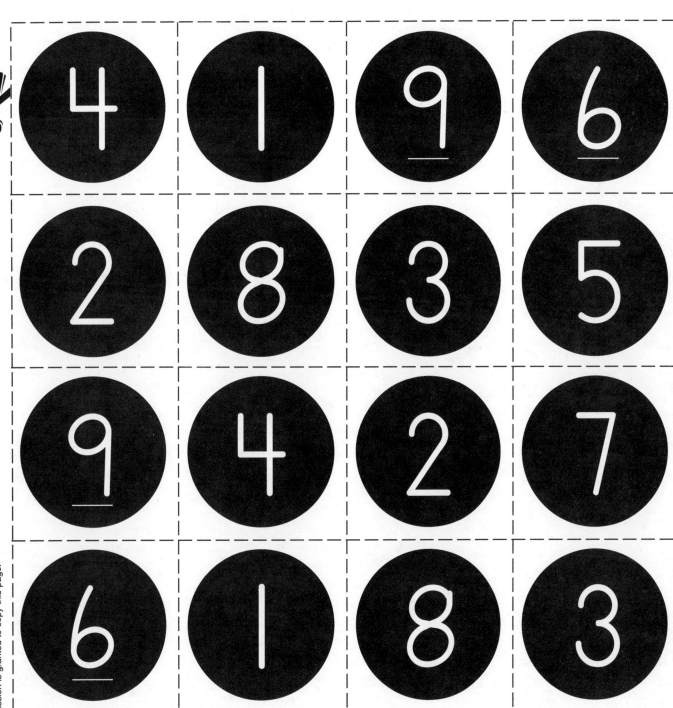

Games to Take Home